MW01043122

FANTASY DESIGNS
COLORING BOOK

AARON POCOCK

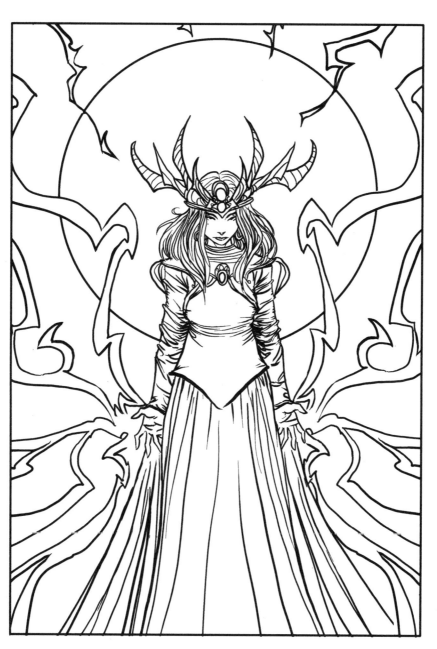

DOVER PUBLICATIONS, INC.
MINEOLA, NEW YORK

This unique coloring collection features elves, giants, dragons, wizards, and more characters from the land of fantasy. The latest edition to Dover's *Creative Haven* series for the experienced colorist, thirty-one highly detailed designs provide you with ample opportunity for experimentation with media and color technique. Plus, the perforated, unbacked pages make displaying your finished work easy.

Bibliographical Note
Fantasy Designs Coloring Book is a new work,
first published by Dover Publications, Inc., in 2015.

International Standard Book Number
ISBN-13: 978-0-486-80128-5
ISBN-10: 0-486-80128-4

Manufactured in the United States by RR Donnelley
80128404   2015
www.doverpublications.com

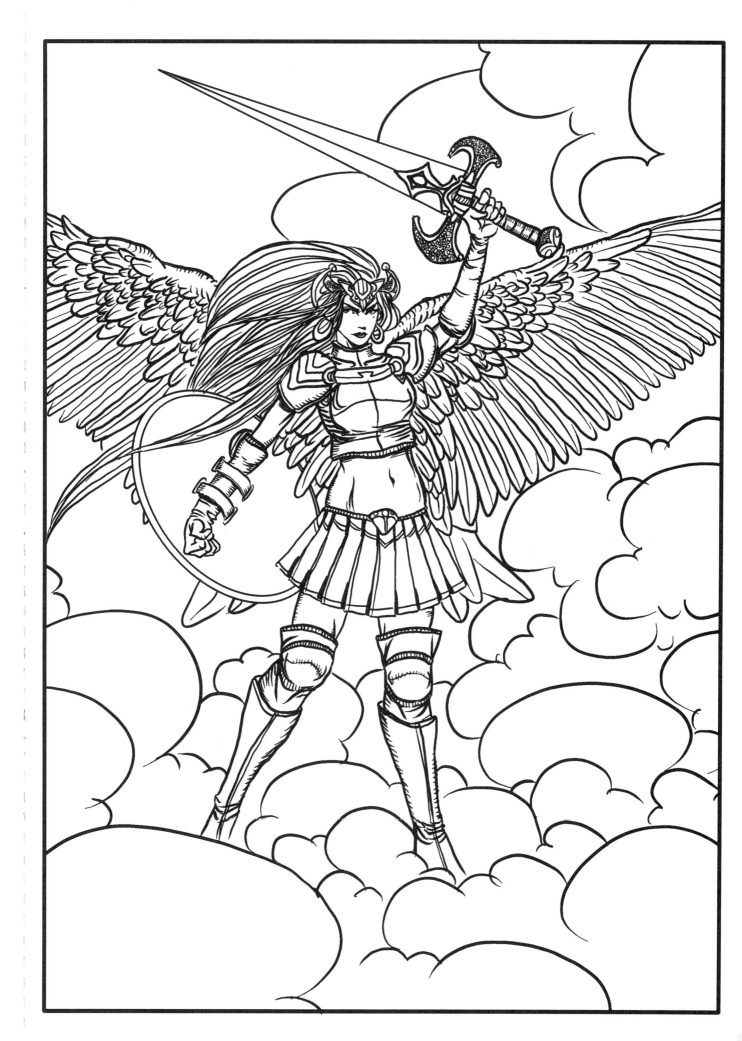

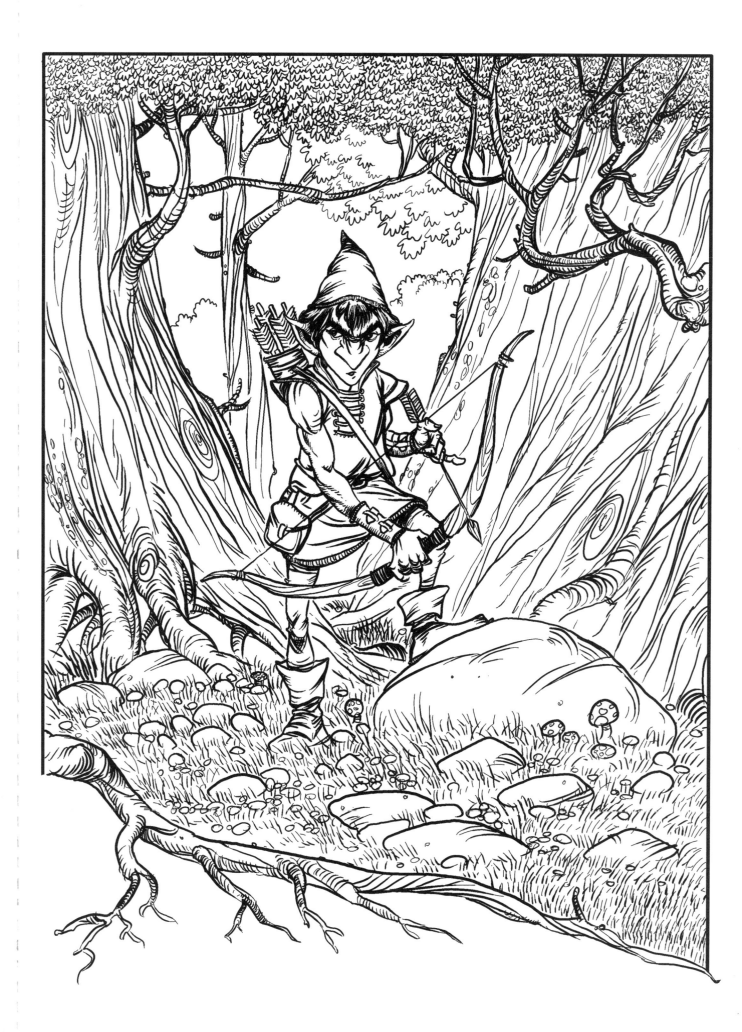

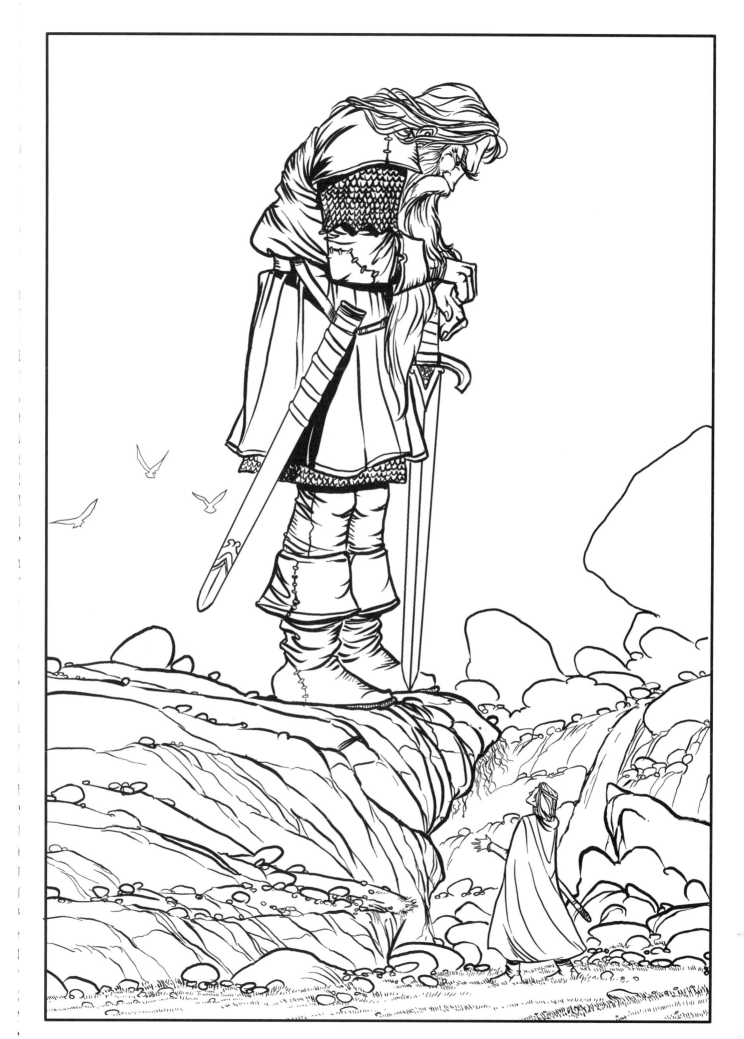

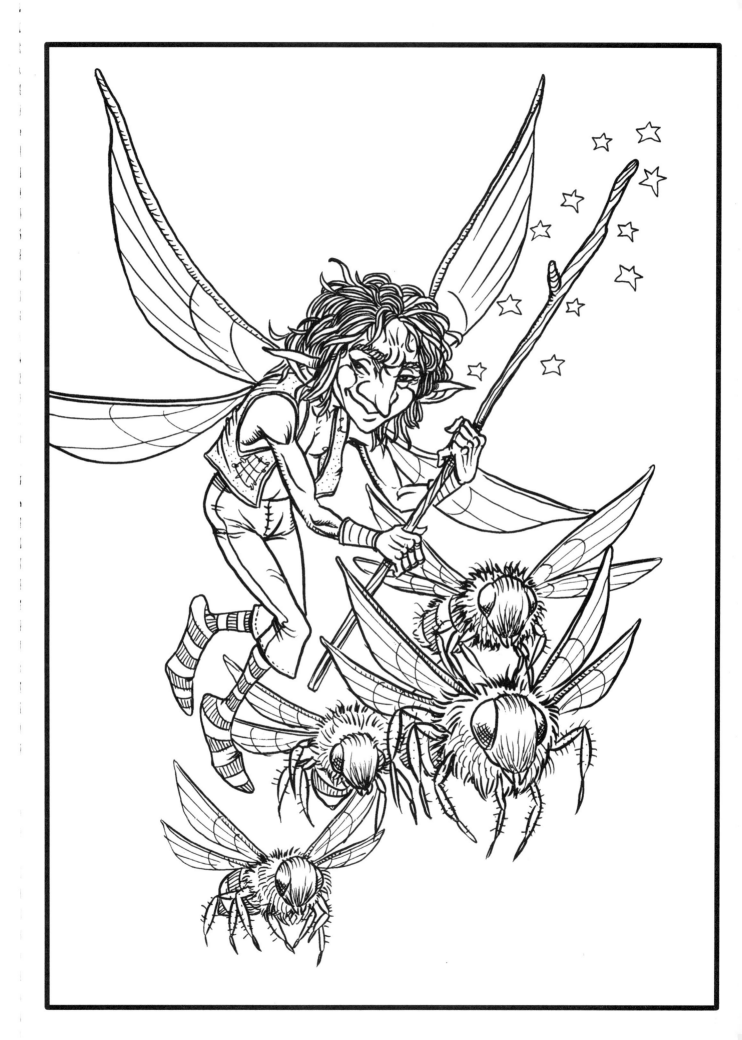

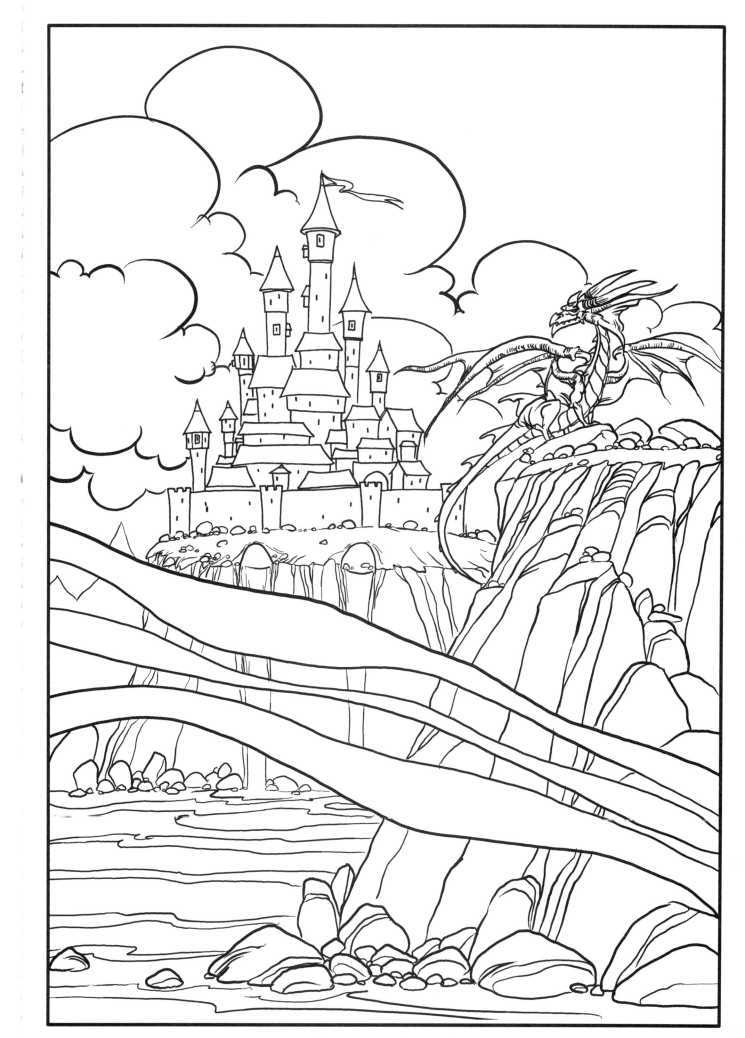

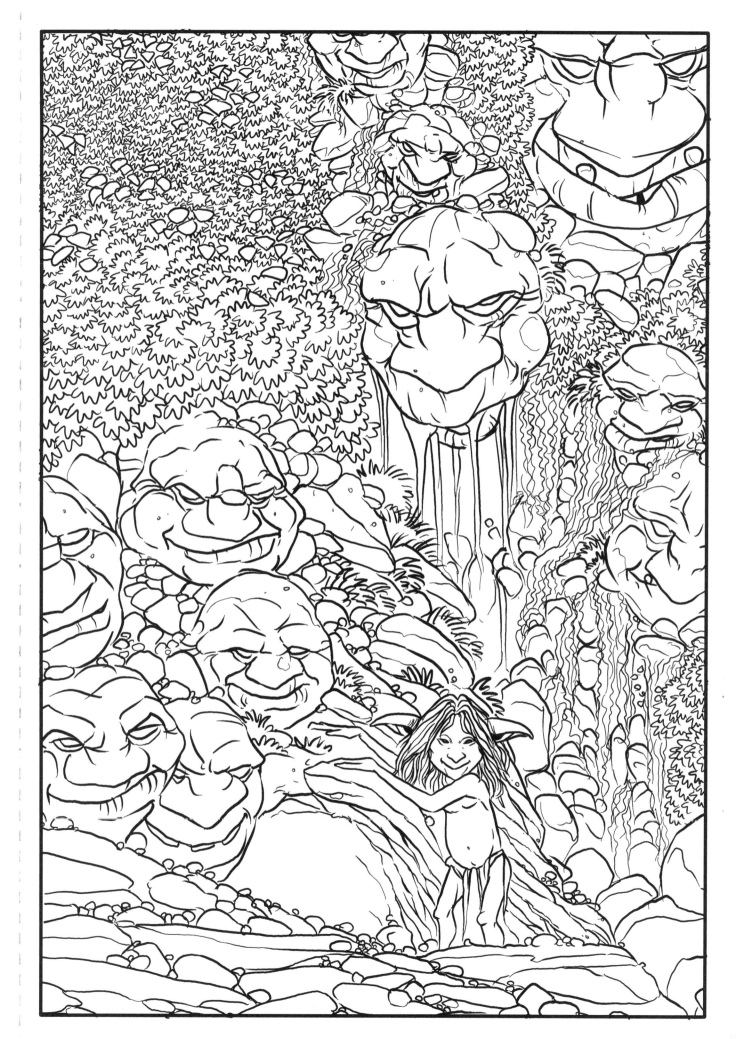

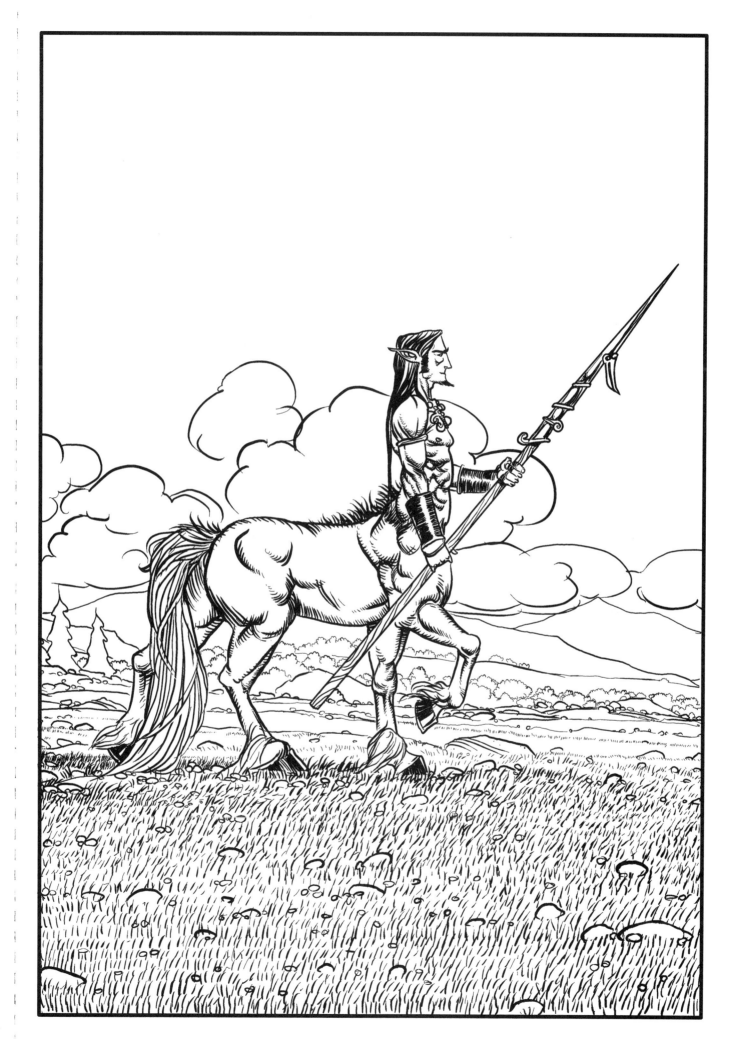

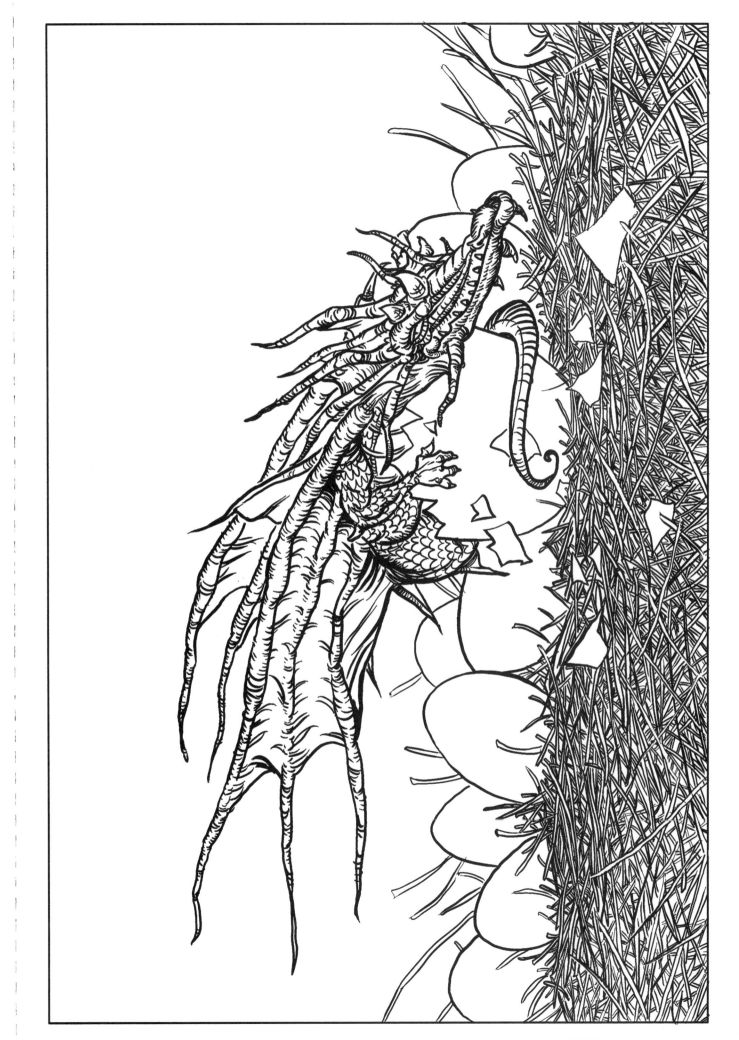

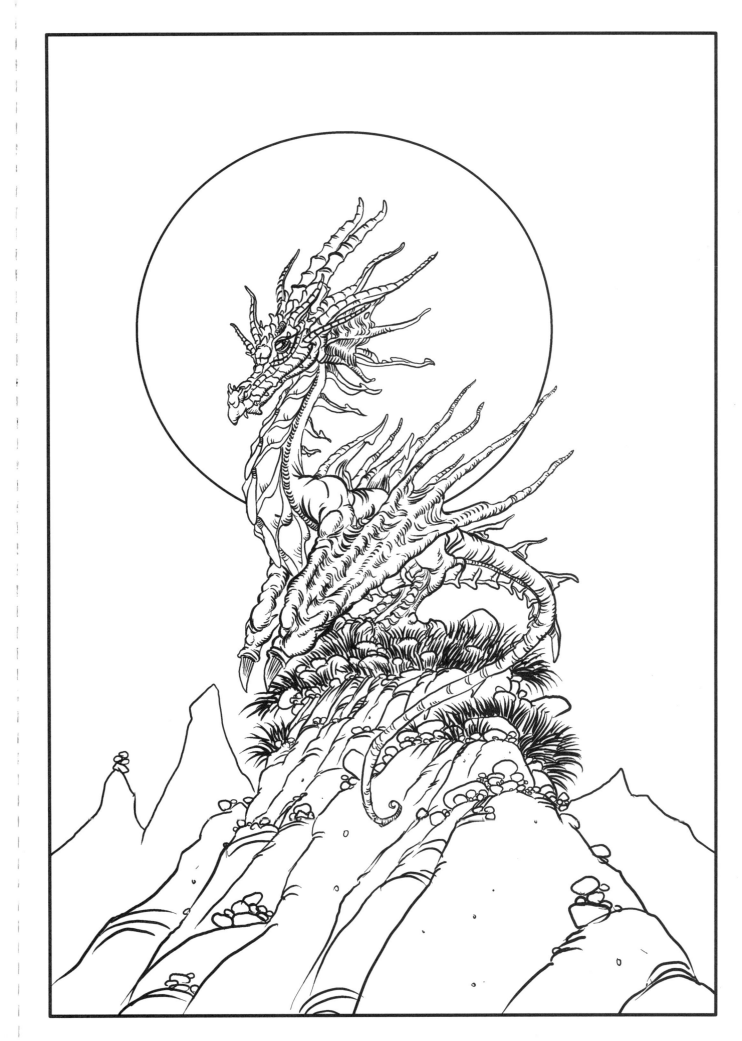

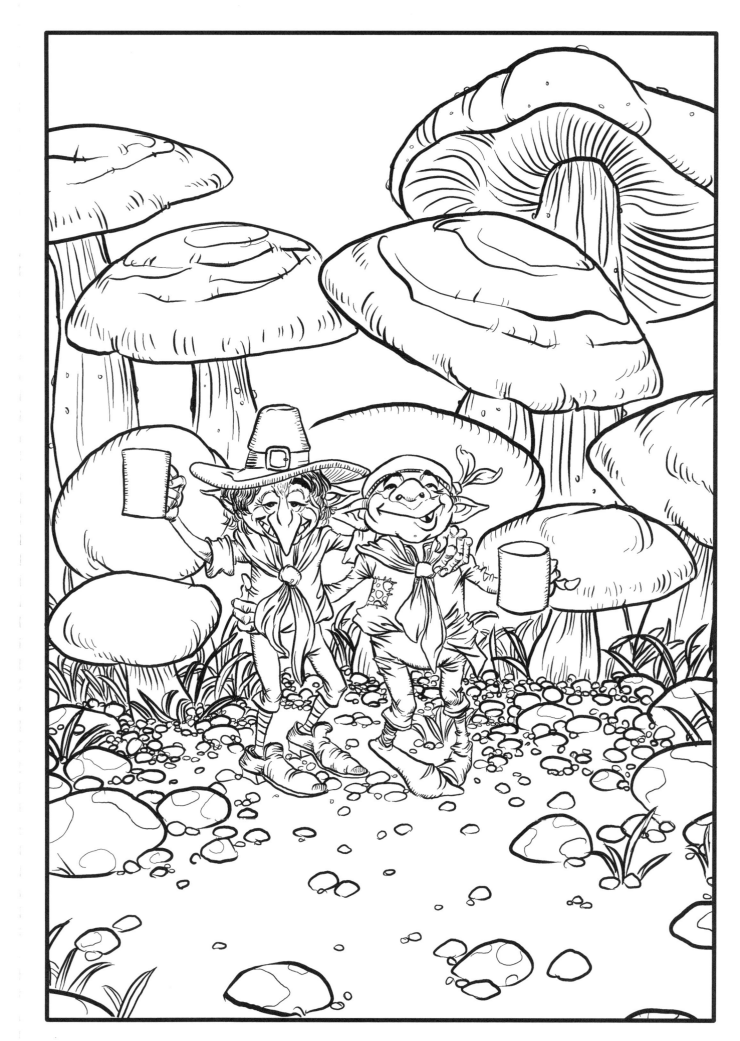

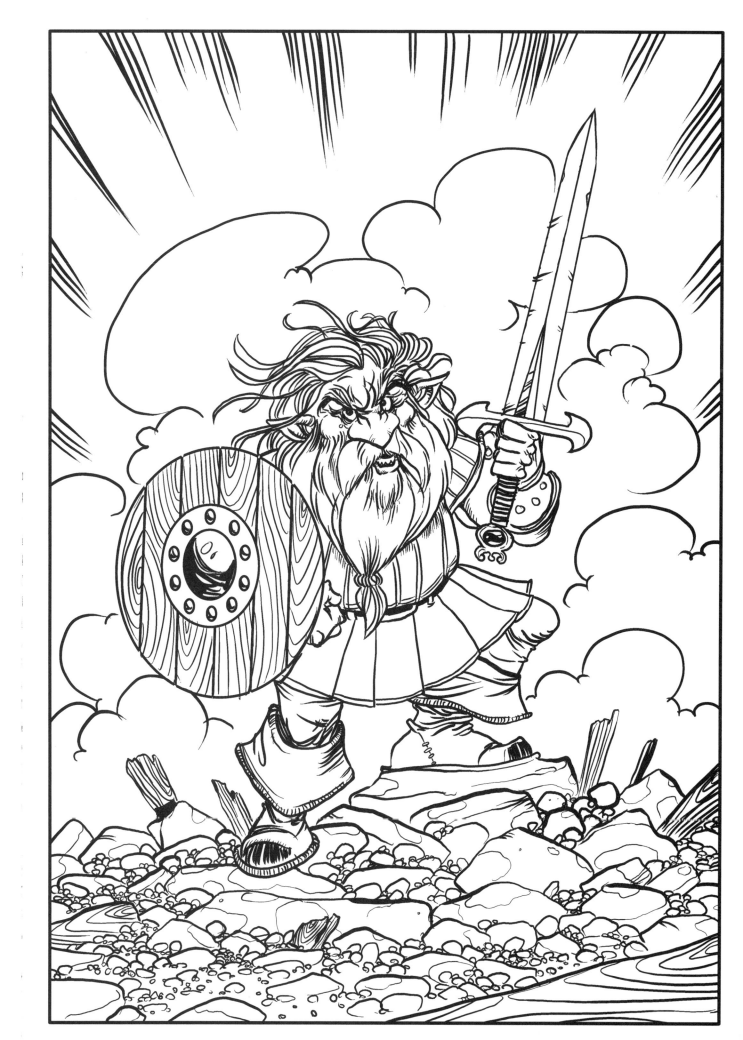

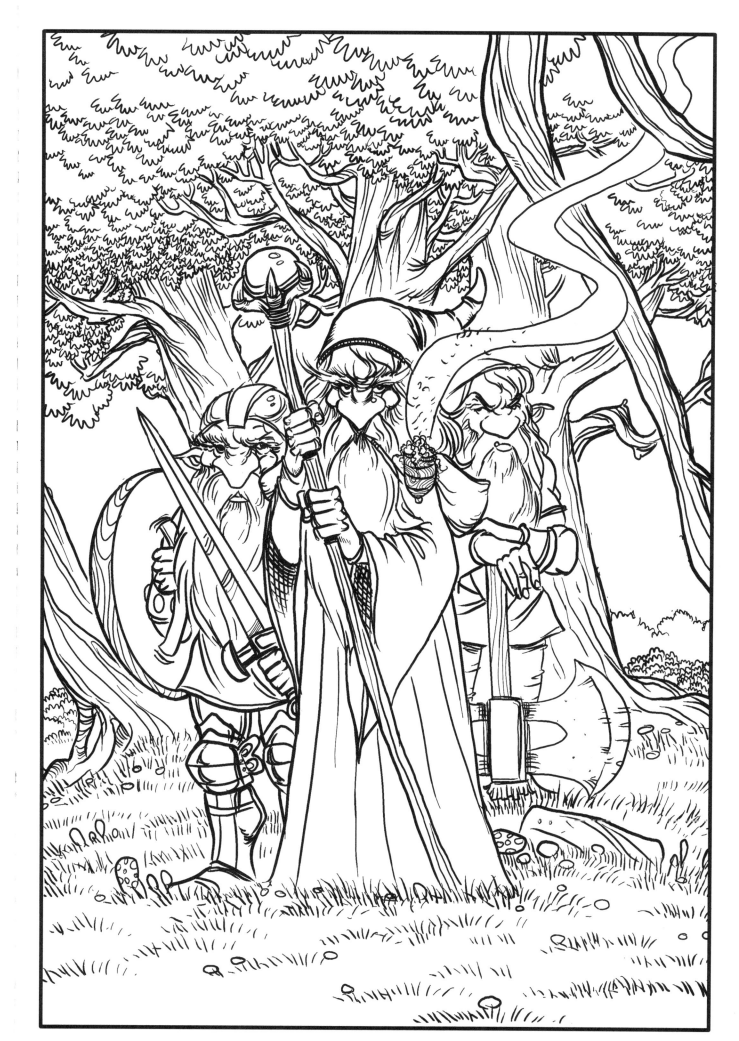

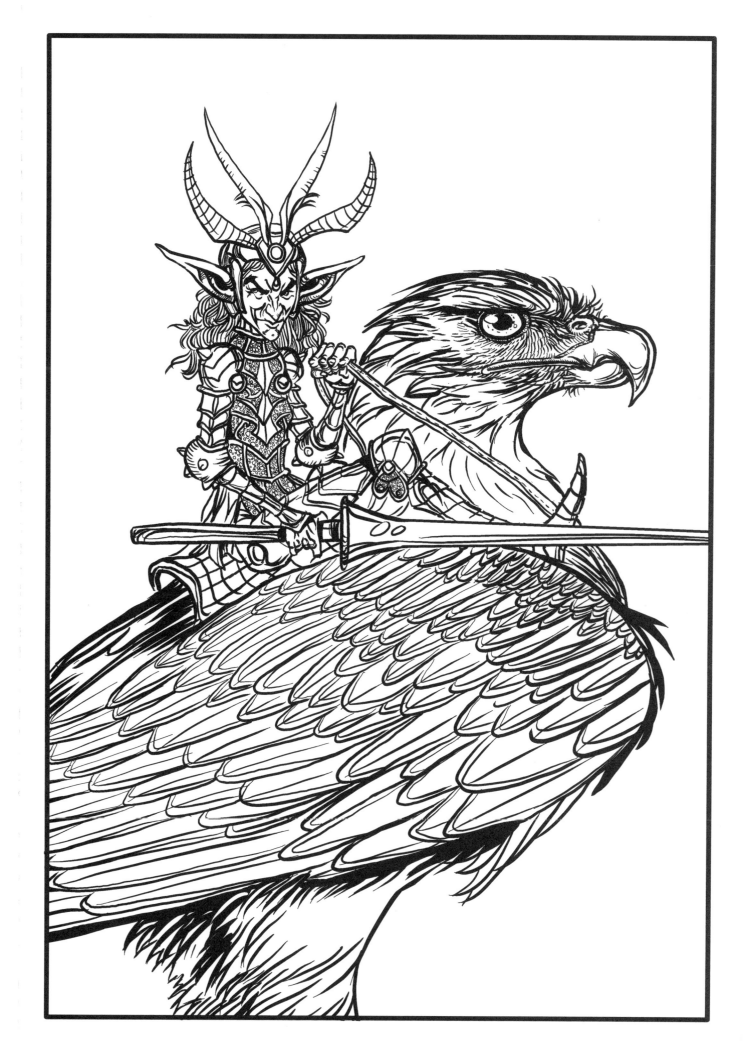

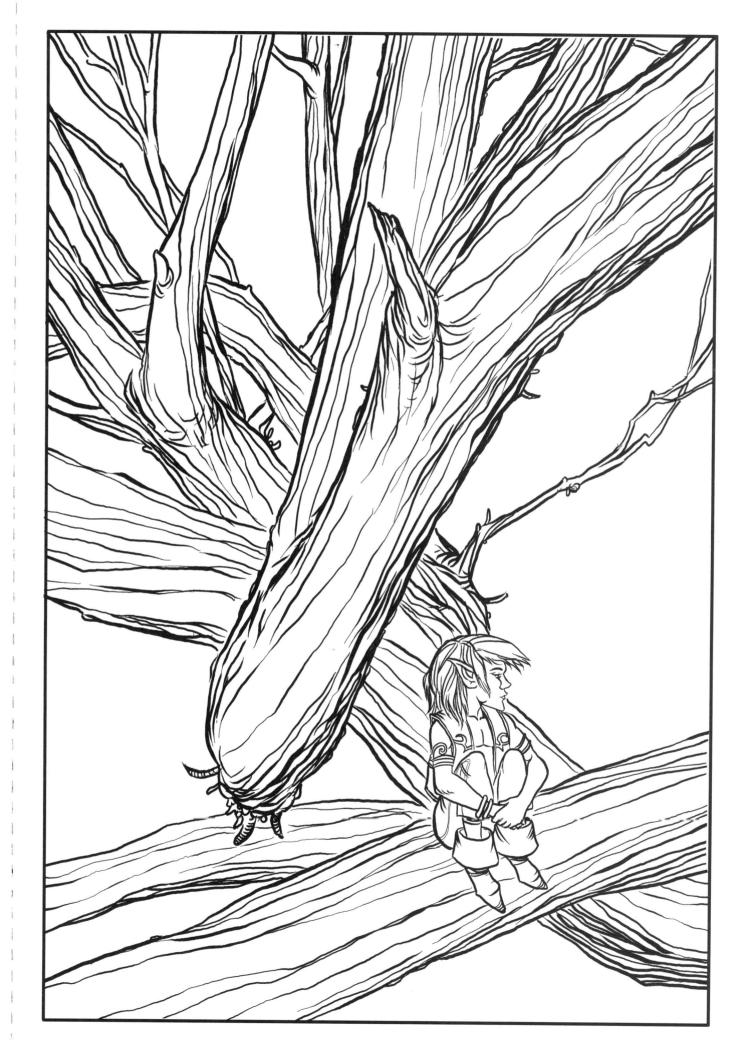

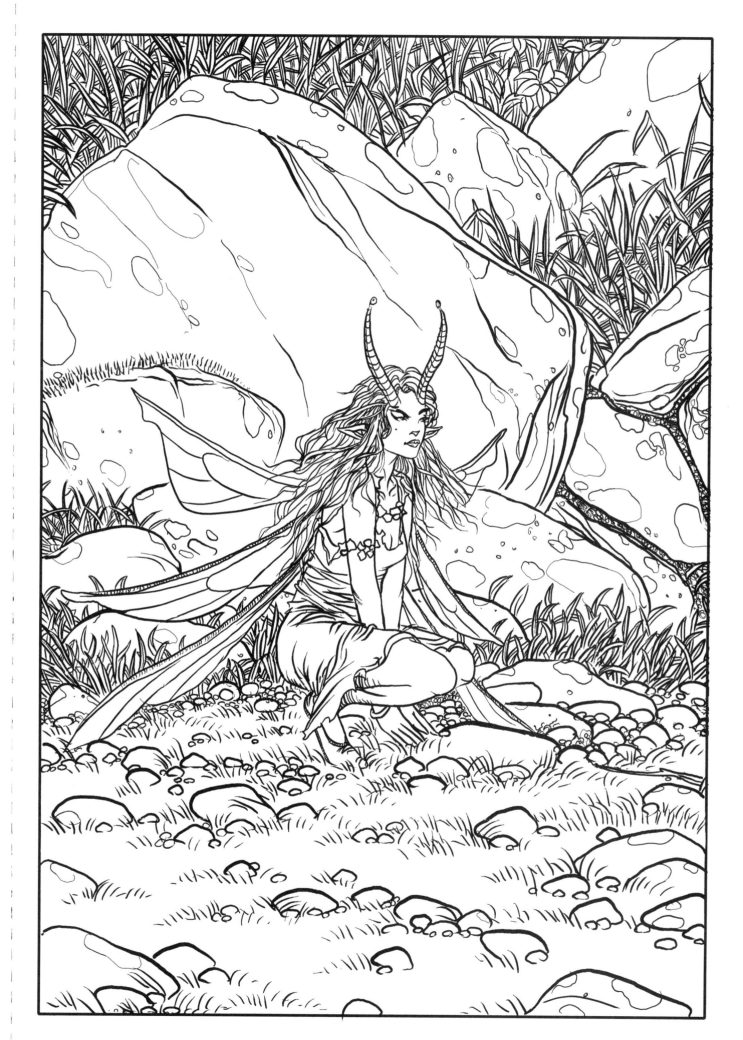

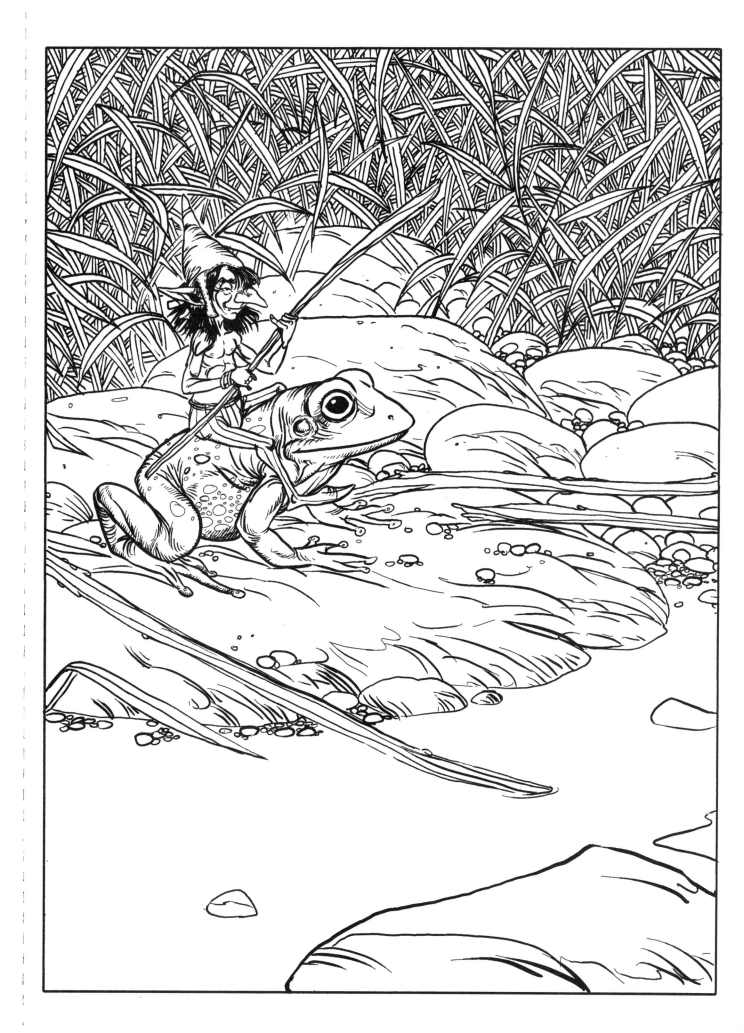

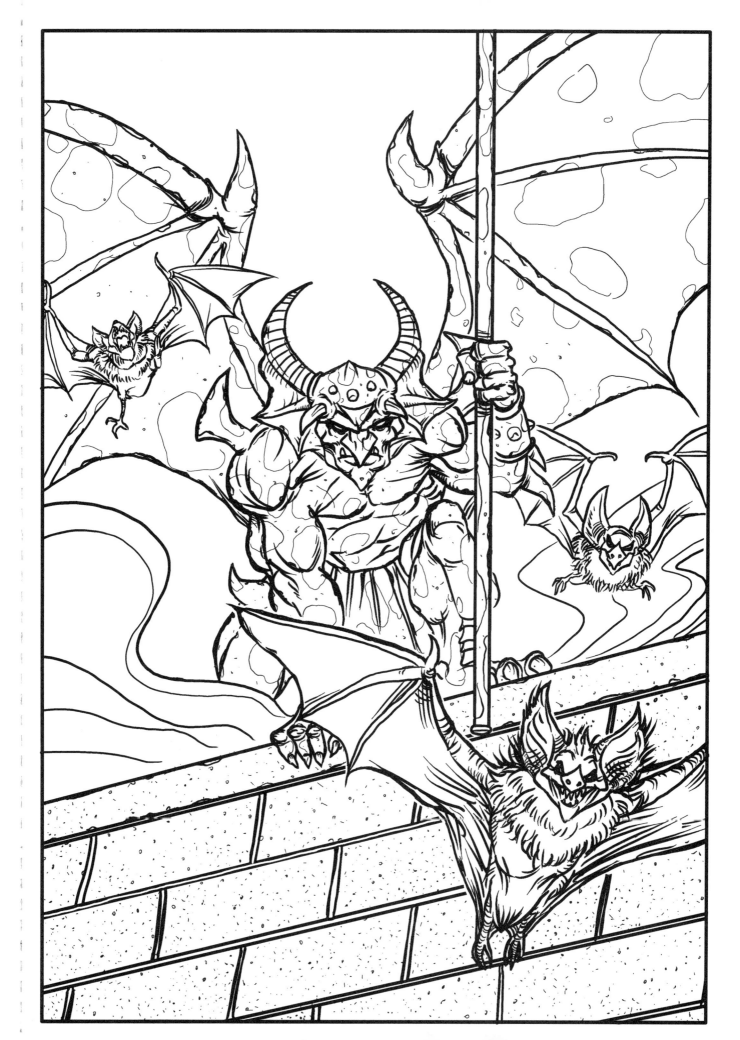

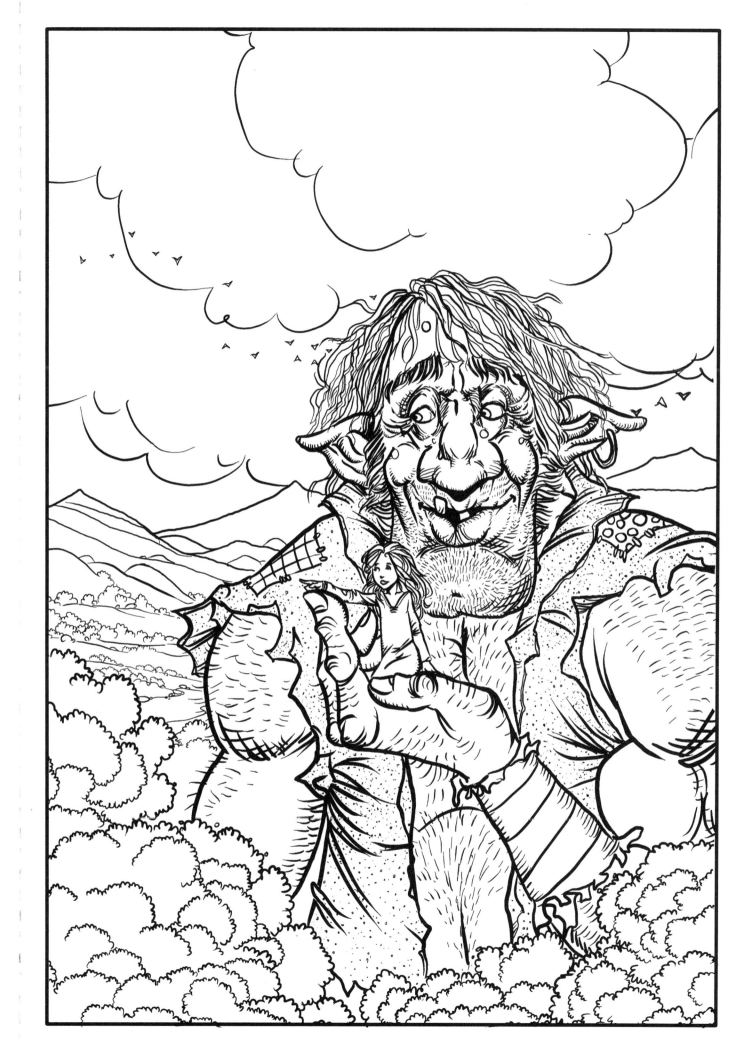

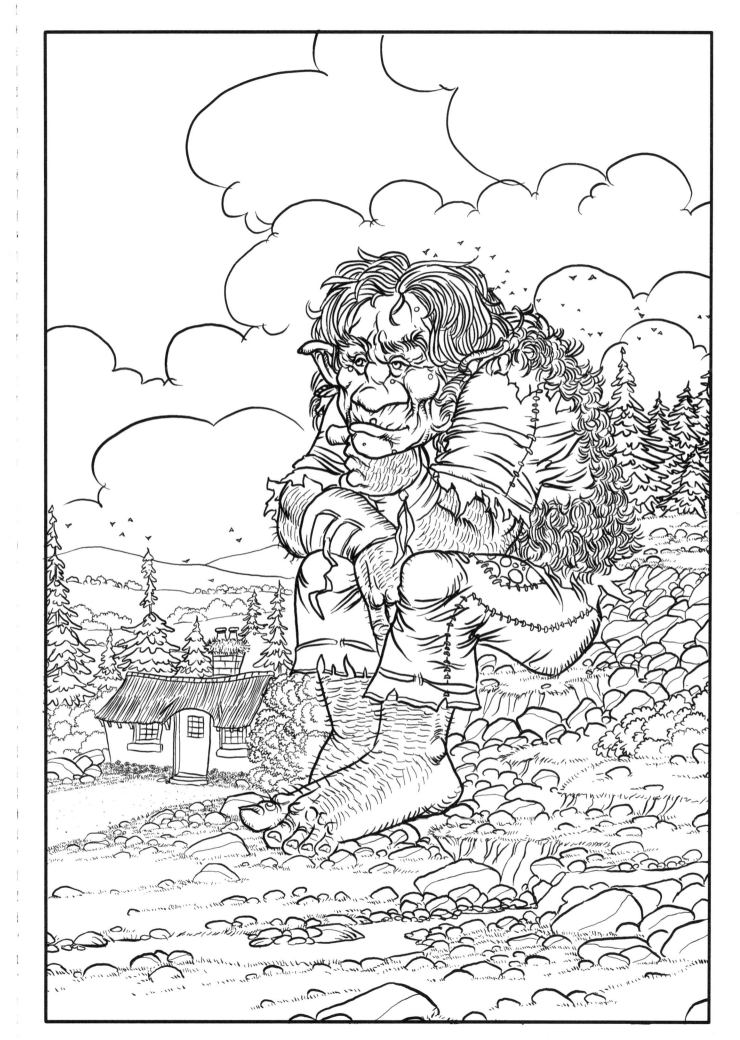

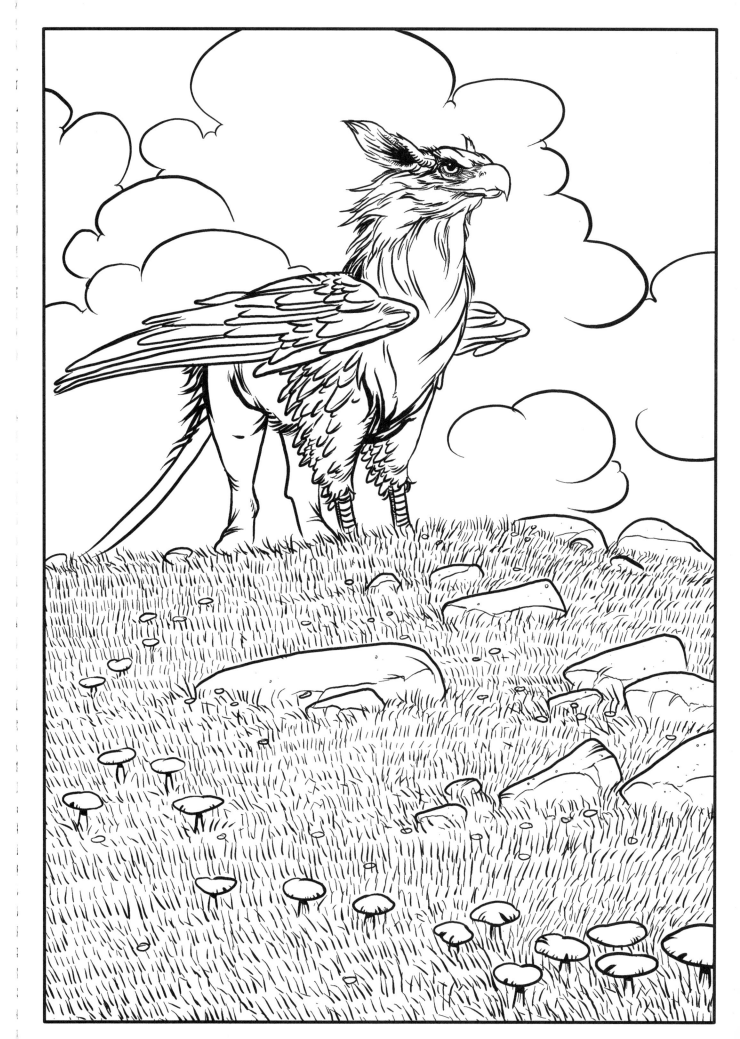

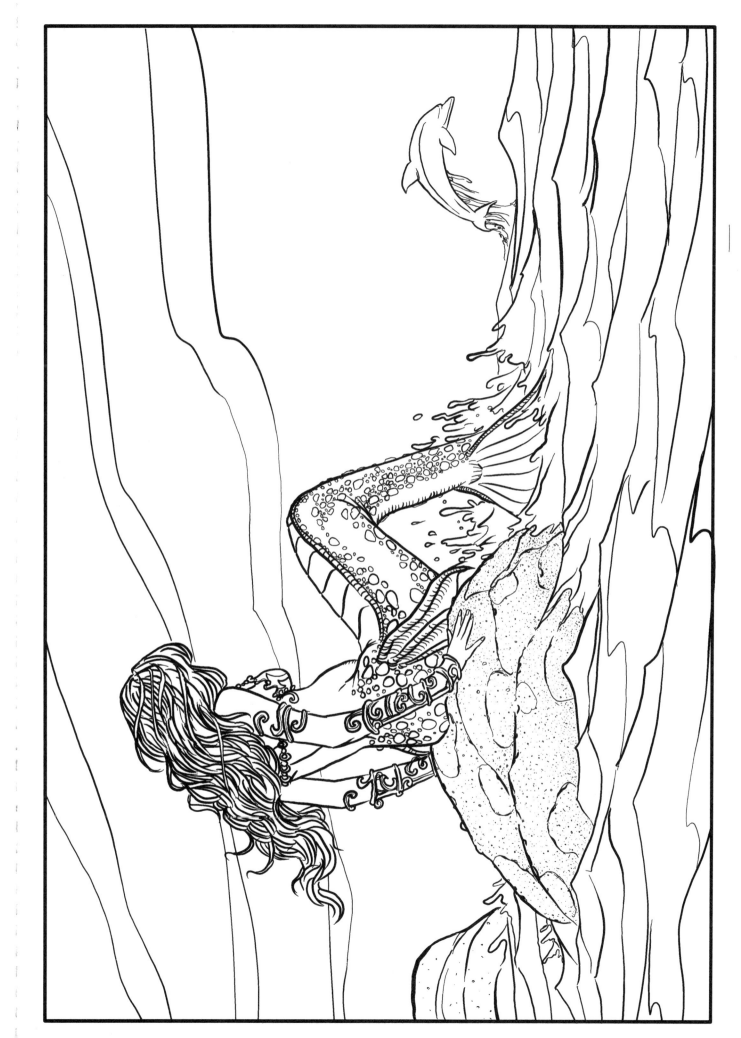

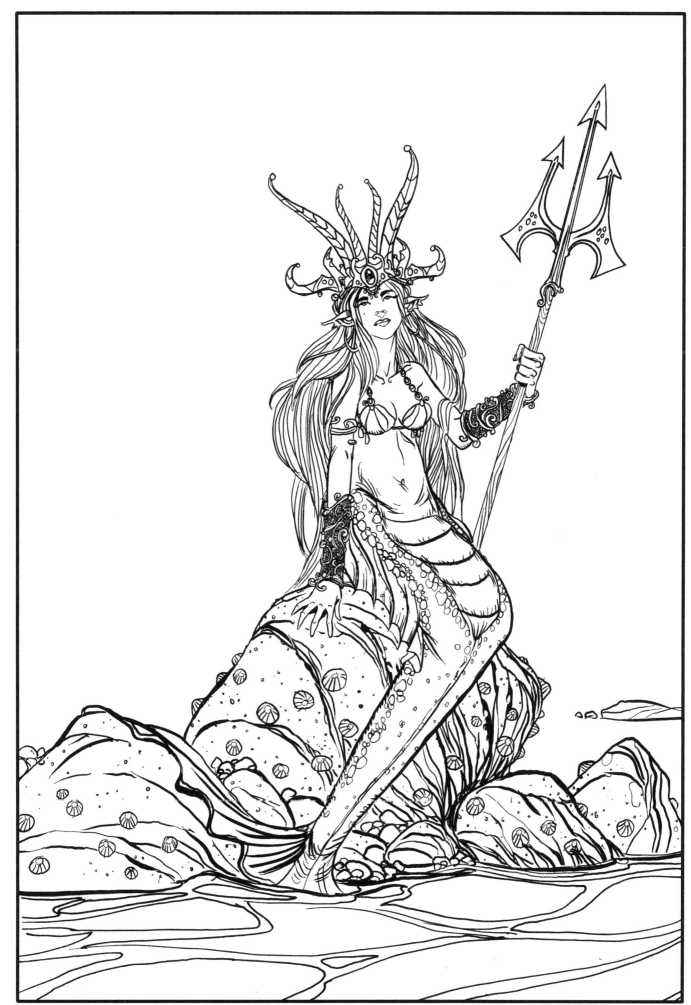

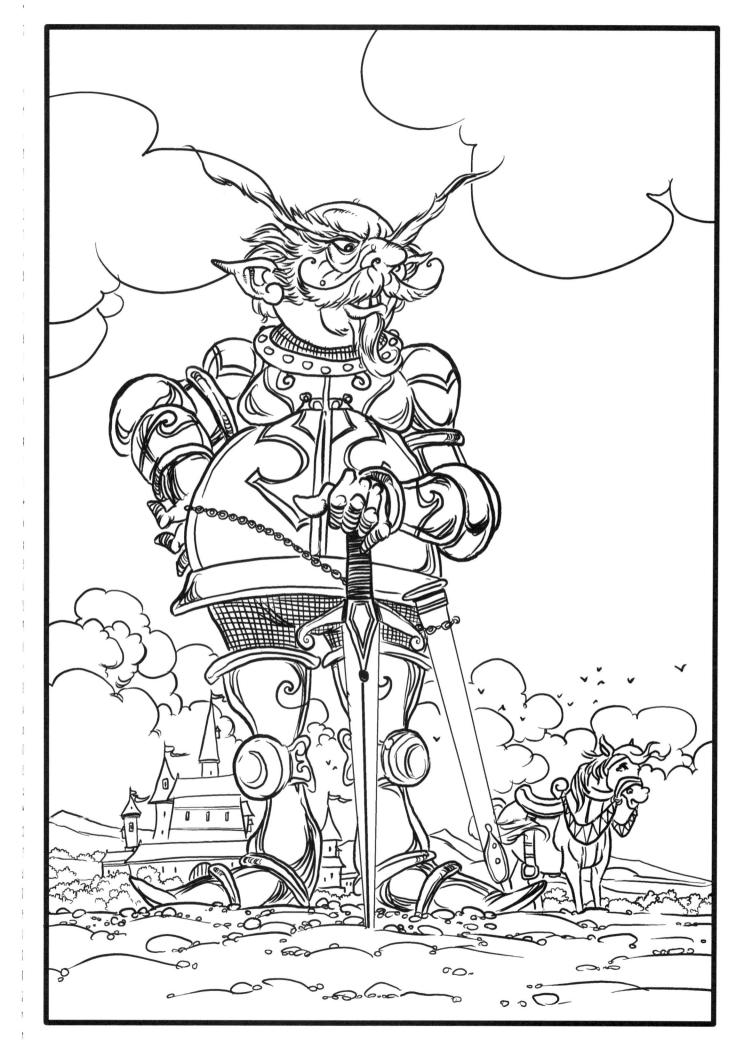

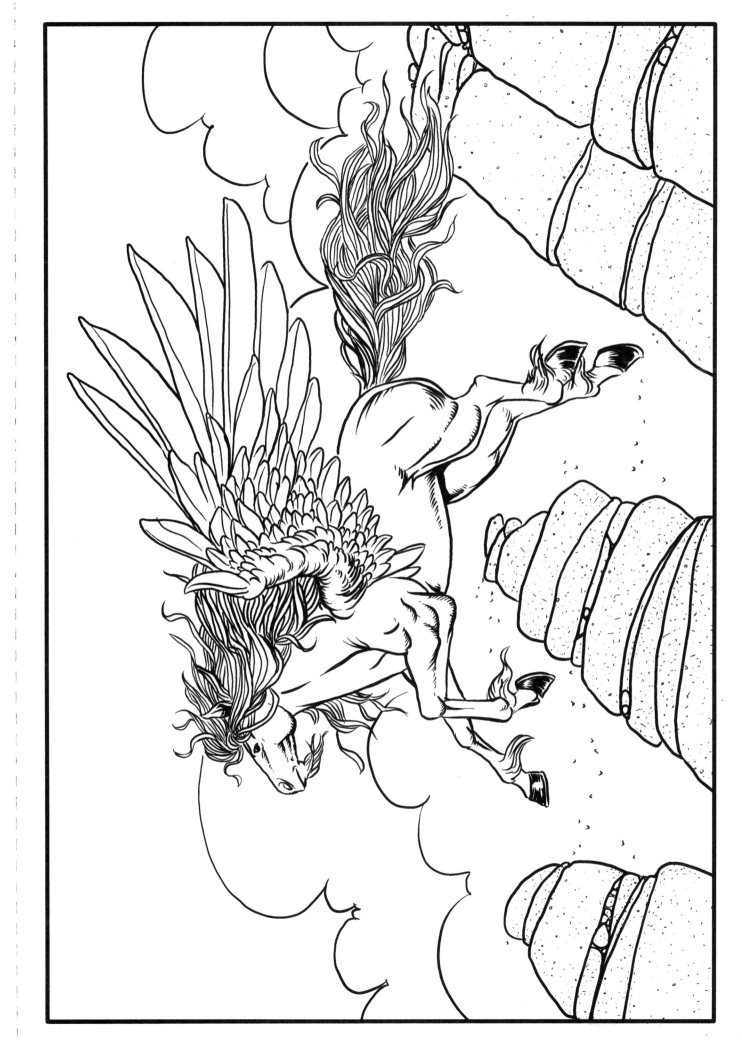

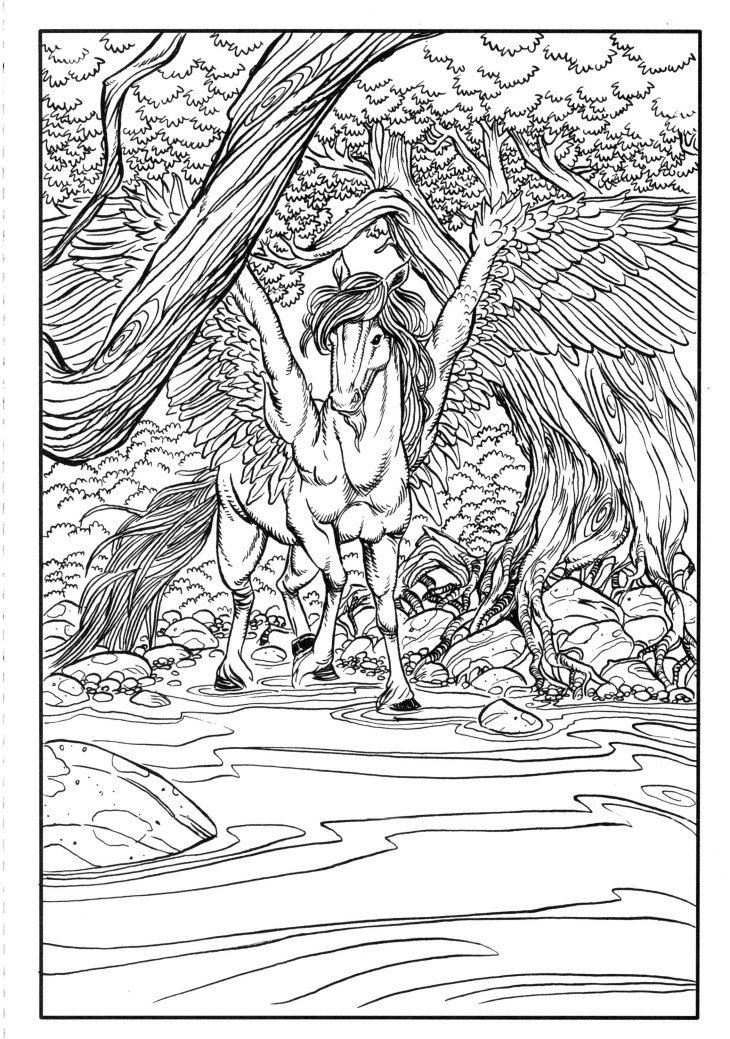

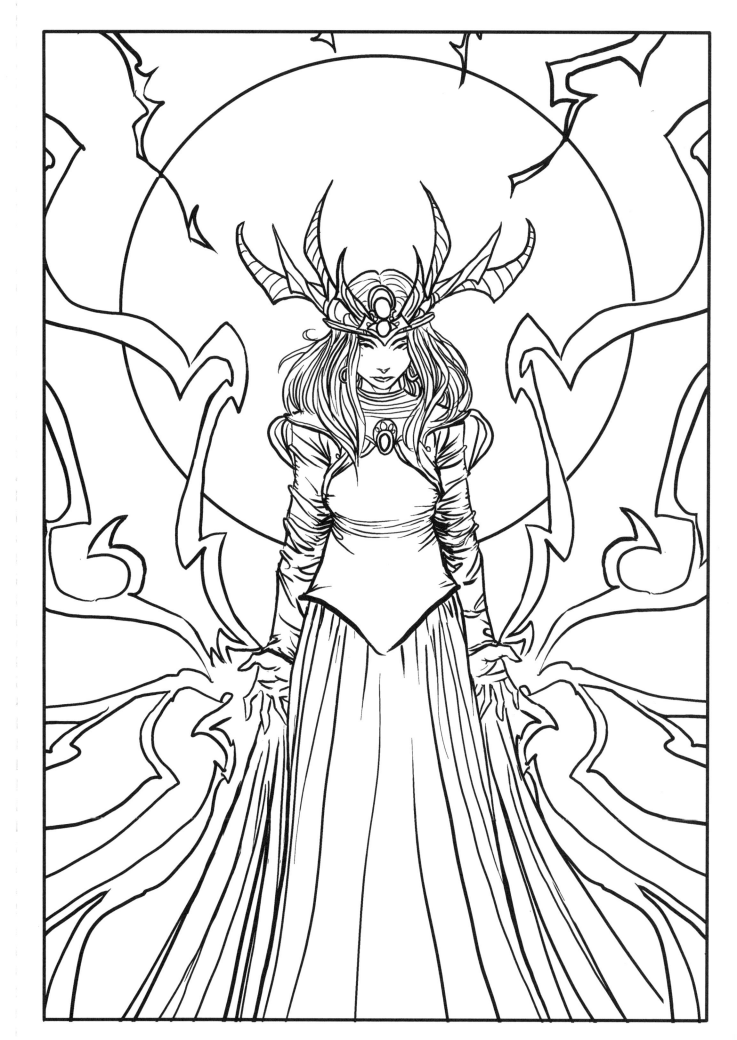

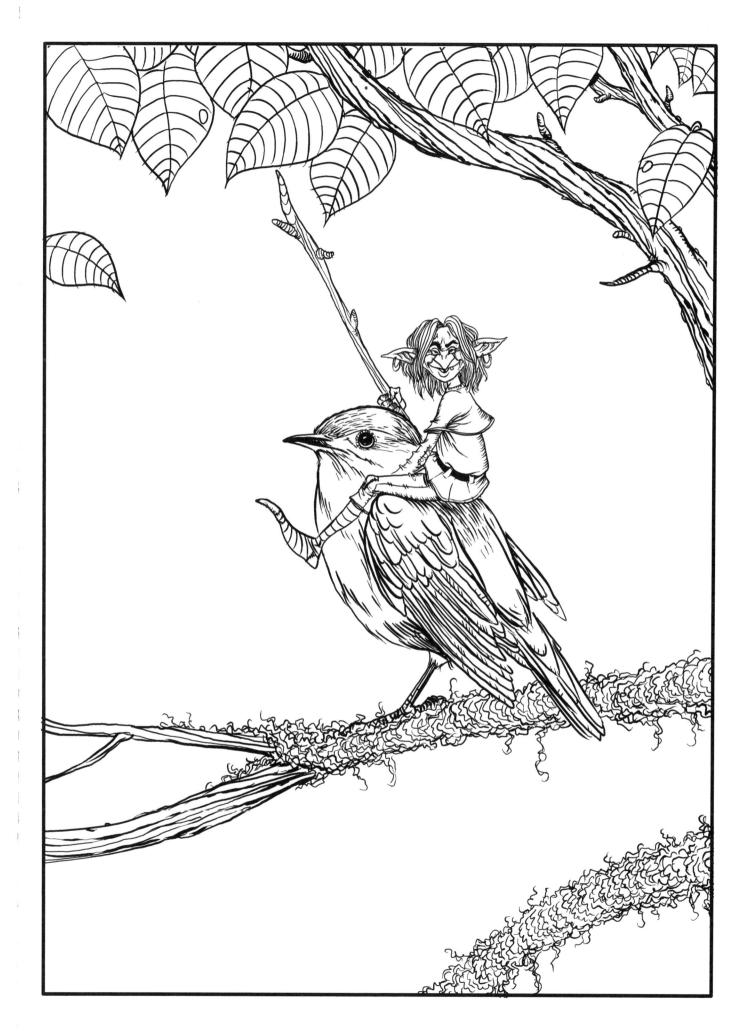

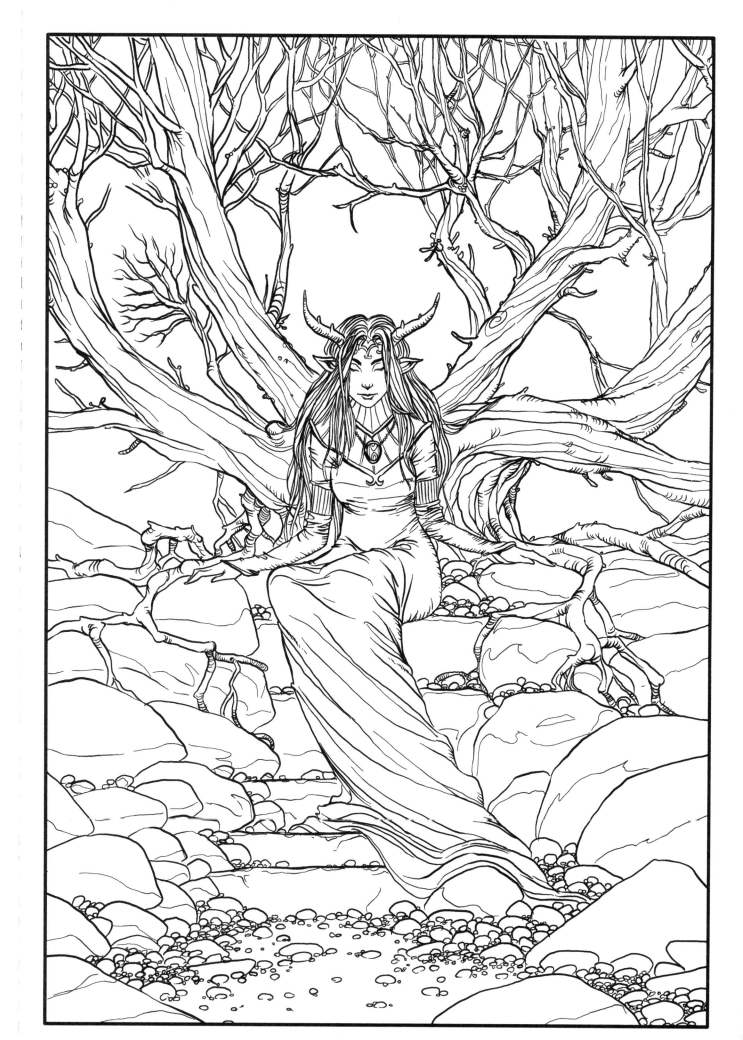

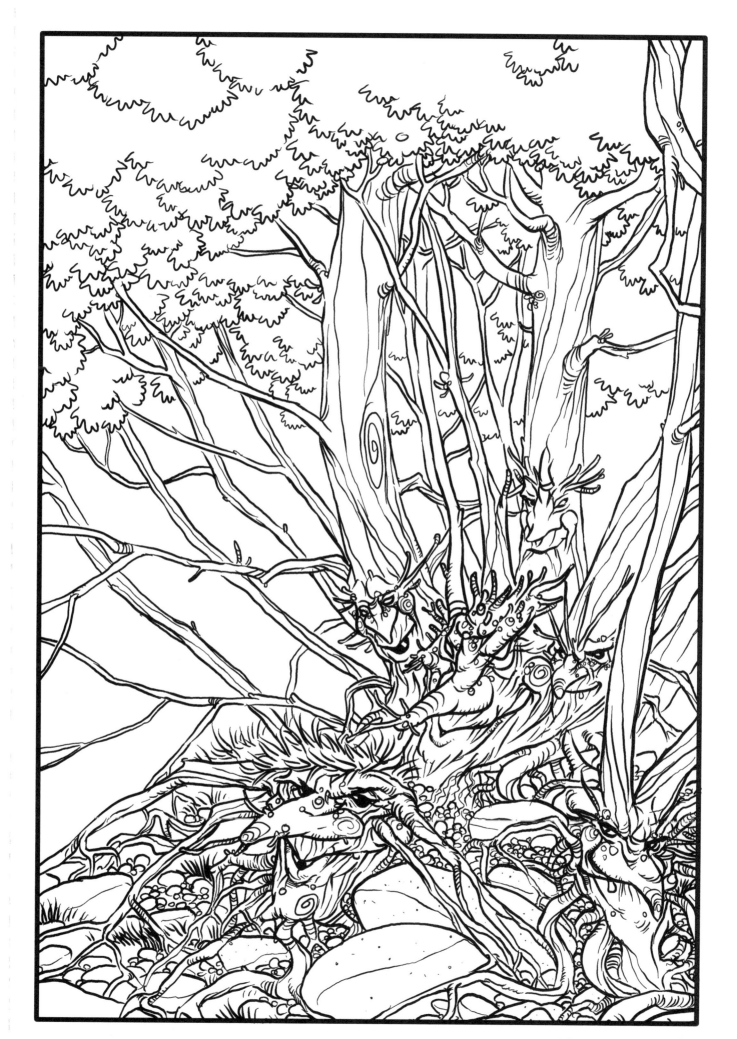

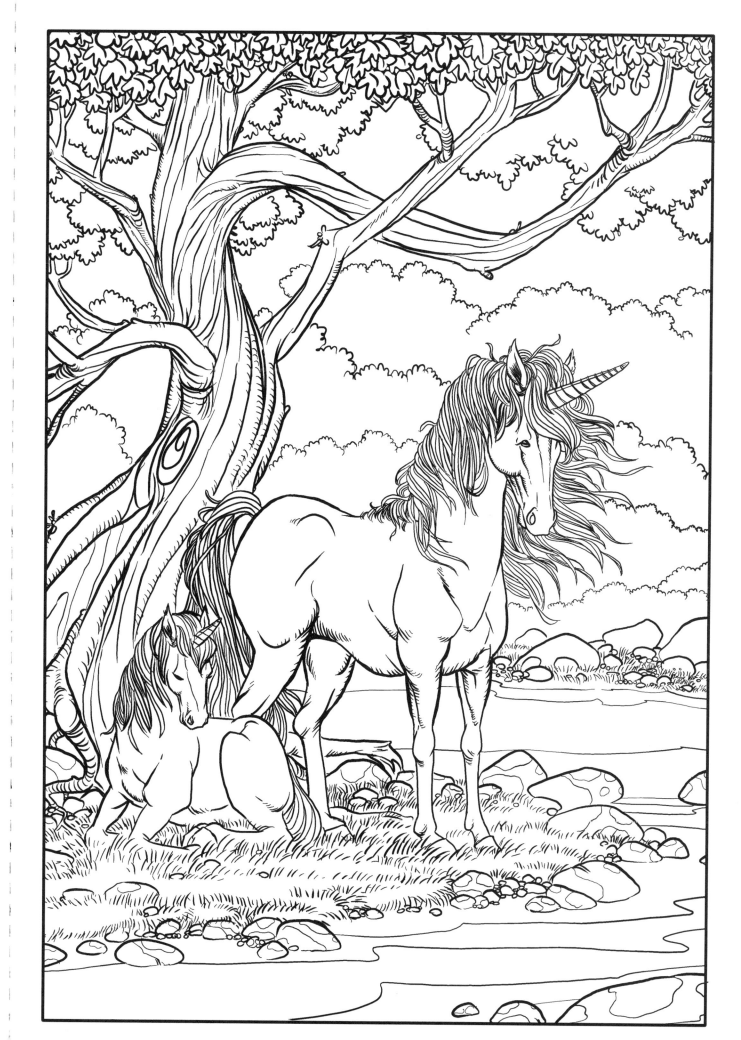

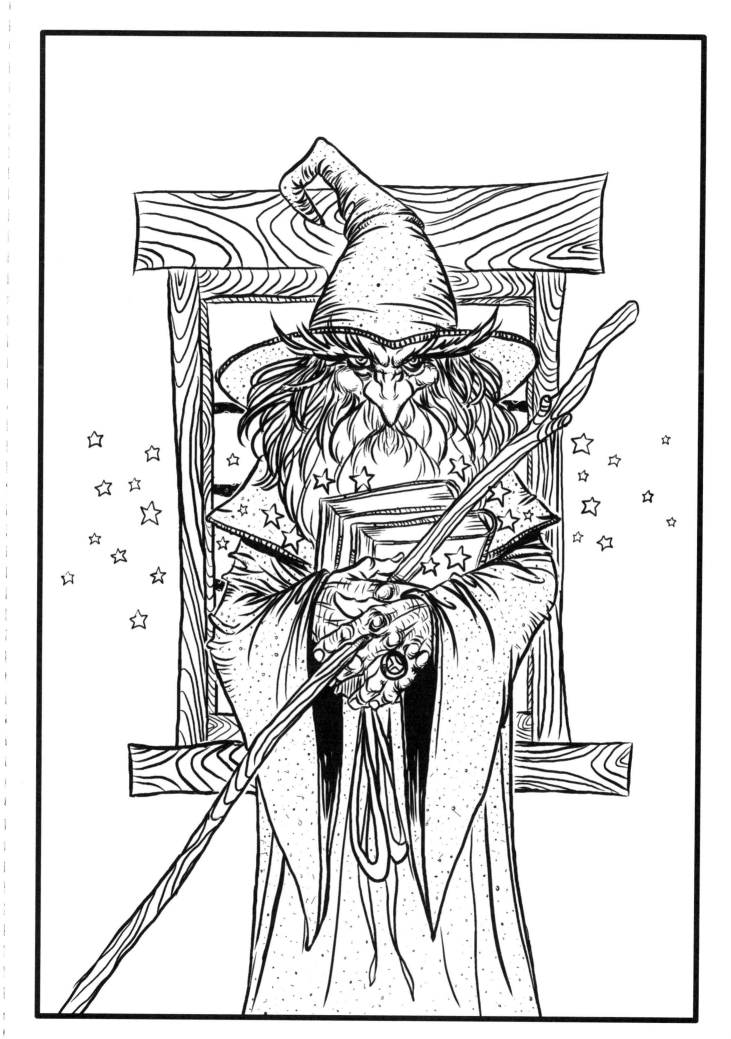